BRITAIN IN PICTURES
THE BRITISH PEOPLE IN PICTURES

ENGLISH DIARIES AND JOURNALS

GENERAL EDITOR
W. J. TURNER

★

The Editor is most grateful to all those who have
so kindly helped in the selection of illustrations,
especially to officials of the various public
Museums, Libraries and Galleries, and
to all others who have generously
allowed pictures and MSS.
to be reproduced

ENGLISH
DIARIES AND JOURNALS

KATE O'BRIEN

WITH
8 PLATES IN COLOUR
AND
19 ILLUSTRATIONS IN
BLACK & WHITE

WILLIAM COLLINS OF LONDON
MCMXXXXIII

PRODUCED BY
ADPRINT LIMITED LONDON

★

PRINTED
IN GREAT BRITAIN BY
WM. COLLINS SONS AND CO. LTD. GLASGOW

SEVENTEENTH CENTURY FRIENDS MEETING HOUSE
In the Time of George Fox

LIST OF ILLUSTRATIONS

PLATES IN COLOUR

BLACK AND WHITE ILLUSTRATIONS

LET me begin with the hard saying that the best English diaries have been written by bores. It will be the purpose of ensuing pages so to illustrate, explain and modify this statement as, I hope, to remove its sting ; but for clarity's sake I must start from it as set down above, for I believe it to be a basic truth about the greatest diarists. A bore has been excellently defined as 'a person who mentions everything.' '*L'art d'ennuyer c'est de tout dire*,' and face to face with us, across the fireplace or the dining table, the exponent of this art is very nearly intolerable ; but at the remove which lies between a writer and a reader, when the 'everything', printed not spoken, is in our power, to be taken or left as we feel inclined, and when distance, time, have given it patina and perspective, he who in life might have been our plague becomes our entertainer, and sometimes more than that—a light, a lamp, a gentle, accidental resurrector for a while of what had been cold and dead.

And it is of course probable, indeed almost certain, that in life this diarist, this entertainer, was *not* a bore, that he escaped the Nemesis of his temperament by the grace of being a diarist; for it is unlikely that a man who noted down in ink everything he saw, heard or otherwise experienced each day over a period of years should have had the vitality or indeed the time to recount himself to his contemporaries *verbatim* as he does to us. So their escape is our gain ; and his adaptation to script of his perpetual need to pettifog and annotate translates the latter into positive merit, and in some cases makes posterity and history immeasurably the debtors of a few eccentric or fussy or over-cautious men who, but for the chance that they scribbled rather than chattered, might have remained for ever obscure to us—just departed bores, mercifully stemmed in the irresponsive grave from their habit of 'running on'.

A good diary is not necessarily literature ; for of its nature it must be free of most of the disciplines and tests of a work of art. Vision, imagination, passion, fancy, invention, scholarship, detachment, and the steely restraints and consciously selected embellishments of form and of design—none of these has a vital place in diary-writing. They break in, it is true, or may do so; but that they are not essential to a diarist or part of his talent is at once his advantage and his peril—his advantage if, apart from them, he possesses enough of the attributes his task *may* demand, for so, merely by pleasing himself and evading all the pains of art, he will come to wear a laurel as evergreen as Pepys'; his peril, too, because any piece of writing, diary or what you will, can only manage to live and get itself read by projecting somehow that illusion of life and truth which is the function of literature. So the diarist might be in a dilemma were he self-conscious along these lines, or posterity-conscious. But he need not worry, very likely; for his impulse—to set down everything—proves his vitality. And vitality, the first and the only unfakeable element of literature, is what he needs above all else for getting read hereafter. Let him be alive, and rock-set on reproducing for us the daily pattern made by his own liveliness—an odd necessity, you may say, in any really lively person, but that is irrelevant—and ten to one you will get a good diary. History and its ironies, the eternal nostalgia of readers and their simple curiosity—all will do for his pages what the creative artist would have had to do for them himself; and out of a minimum of effort and a maximum of self-indulgence, something which is almost a work of art may be observed to grow, to have grown.

In the simplicity therefore with which the typical English diarist sets out to capture on paper the busy to and fro of his earthly span lies the threat of his being by nature a bore. For, if we except journals kept in special circumstances—as for instance in the course of perilous explorations such as Captain Scott's, or say Wesley's enormous and businesslike record of his missions—there is something a touch complacent and niggling in the design. And it is true that so far as we know almost no really great man has been in the normal course of his life a consistent diary-keeper. André Gide is a curious exception, and we must hope that he is still industriously and resolutely proving the rule—for our future enlightenment and delight. And we shall never know what journals and notebooks many of the great have had the wit, or the folly, to throw into the fire. But, as the records stand and as the diaries have come down to us, they are provedly not a form of self-expression which has appealed to the richly endowed. They are the medium of secondary types, as a rule—the outlet of the modest, the orderly and, sometimes, the complacent.

And they are none the worse for that. Indeed, paradoxically, their greatness, or more accurately, their great value lies now in their littleness, their concern with the passing day and the particular—the price of a dish of Tongue and Udder, the effect of a rhubarb purge, the writing of a postcard. Diarists have found such matters worth the setting down—

WILLIAM DUGDALE 1605-1686
Oil painting by an unknown artist
By courtesy of the Curators of the Bodleian Library

The Navy Office London

THE NAVY OFFICE, CRUTCHED FRIARS, LONDON, WHERE PEPYS HAD HIS OFFICE

Coloured engraving published by T. Taylor, 1714

which means that had they not set them down they would have pestered their contemporaries with them—and been bores of the kind we all know, who labour the obvious, and teach grandmother to suck eggs.

Trivia of custom, of gossip or of comment could not of themselves, of course, sustain a diary, or give it importance ; but the diarist's necessity of writing them down places them, willy-nilly, in relation to large things and gives them as it were their function of accent or balance in the composition of a period ; time itself heightens this function ; and in the greater diaries the writer, managing to relate his very self to his notes and his doings, managing actually to express his own life, however modest or however brilliant, in just proportion to his time, does arrive, even if haphazardly, at creating one kind of work of art. So we may fall upon the irony of the little man of little talent and less ambition accomplishing, in conspiracy with time, such strokes of illumination, of irony or of sheer, true life as the great imaginative ones have always had to wrestle for in uncertainty and pain, and with all their faculties on the stretch. Thus it is, perhaps, when Nancy Woodforde writes down, as dully and smugly as possible, on Friday Sept. 28th, 1792, in a Norfolk parsonage : 'Mr and Mrs Custance sent us a brace of partridges. Dreadful times in France. Many are fled for refuge here.' That placid entry shows us as neatly as it could be done how wide and green and safely misted were then as for a long time afterwards the miles that lay between historic inevitabilities and that constant of rural England, the provincial lady. And when Francis Kilvert writes, on March 7th, 1873 : 'As I walked home across the meadows the sun was sinking low. In the clear beautiful evening a bird-hunting boy with a light heart was singing at the top of his voice across the fields. I only caught snatches of the verses. It seemed to be a love-song, and he repeated the same lines again and again. When he had ended his song the boy relieved his feelings by a shout and then sang "Saturday Night is soon a-coming" '—we have a particular spring evening, its sound, its stillness, its essence, related—by a boy's voice across a field—to a hundred such evenings we have known. For that is one thing the diary, at its best, can do—not merely inform us about life, but, by chance fusion of some inner or outer facet of it with what we also know or feel, make us recognise it.

If I seem arbitrary in the pages that follow, I hope I shall be forgiven ; for I take my task to be the pleasant one of discussing my own preferences and dislikes among diarists, rather then gravely and detachedly to compose a concise history of the diary. I shall skip, I shall ignore ; perhaps, should any such glance my way, I shall get into trouble with a scholar or two ; and indeed it might save time for some readers were I forthwith to put my cards on the table and, since what I am about to write will be no more than a record of personal taste, confess at once my chief reaction to the most celebrated of all diaries ? But no—let us begin at the beginning, and hold as nearly as we can to the only order it is practicable to impose on so brief a sketch of a vastly diversified minor art—a loosely chronological one. Let us for simplicity's sake review English diarists and their diaries century by century, as they come.

The English Diary proper seems to have made its first appearance in the seventeenth century. Sir William Dugdale, an industrious Warwickshire gentleman, who laboured all his long life at works of antiquarianism and of heraldry and fought for Charles I in the Civil War, kept a journal during the latter forty-five of his eighty-two years of life which, dull, dry and broken as it is, the merest jotting indeed—'Queene impeached of Treason. Two regiment of foote came from York to Newark.' 'Two sunnes appeared this day.' 'King Charles the 2nd departed this life, about noon.' —does build up, slow stroke by stroke, a portrait of a man. A dull man, unremarkable, inarticulate, hide-bound, yet one faithful alike to his duties and to his interests, having unity in him, and with his conventions tempered by a carefully ordered individualism. In fact, from dry, modest notes never intended for publication, notes localised and made small by the writer's phlegmatic temperament even when they touch on large events, we get a reliable portrait—neither inspired nor grossly out of drawing, but merely faithful—of the English country gentleman as he has persisted through three hundred years. Domestic and orderly as well as conventional and idiosyncratic—for Sir William's very last note is simply this : 'Payd Elizabeth Taylor for her Quarter's Wages, now ended, and she going away from us . . .' It is an entry we are to read again and again through the diaries of three hundred years. But Sir William also left us this hearsay note, for January 30th, 1649 : 'The King beheaded at the gate of Whitehalle . . . His head was thrown downe by him yt tooke it up ; bruised ye face. His haire cut of. Souldiers dipped their swords in his blood. Base language upon his dead body.'

When very near the end of his life this modest diarist crossed with a greater, and thus got his name recorded in such a full and broad-flung journal as he could never have attempted. For May 21st, 1685, John Evelyn begins his entry: 'I dined at my Lord Privy Seal's, with Sir William Dugdale, Garter King-at-Arms, author of the *Monasticon* and other learned works ; he told me he was 82 years of age and had his sight and memory perfect . . .'

John Evelyn was a man so gifted, so prosperous, so balanced, so long-lived, so popular, so sane and so naturally self-confident that the average human being may be forgiven if he turns from the bright prospect with something like a shudder. 'A strain of innocent gaiety and refined enjoyment marks Evelyn's life from first to last,' says one commentator. 'Innocent gaiety' is an attractive phrase, but it is open to the neutral reader of

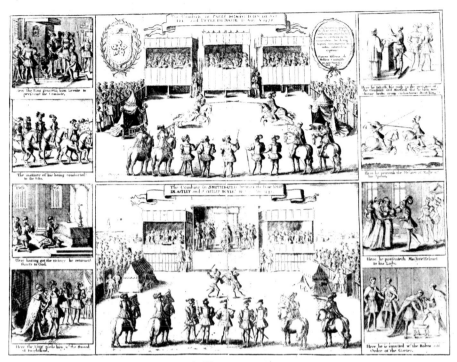

A TOURNAMENT

Engraving from William Dugdale's *Antiquities of Warwickshire*. Second Edition, 1730

the great journal to question its accuracy in description of the gentlemanly shrewdness, the balanced worldliness, which dominate John Evelyn's every page. For my own part, while conceding the 'refined enjoyment,' of which there is a remarkable plenty, I withhold the former tribute as too free and luminous for what it praises. It is captious, maybe, to quarrel however mildly with eighty-five years lived so gracefully, on a high level of learning, taste, piety, good temper and tolerance—yet one cannot but feel that Evelyn's life opened more sweetly and freely, and in greater spiritual and individual promise, than he later understood, or looked for. In 1641, when he was twenty-one, he began the diary which he was to keep with fidelity during sixty-four full and exemplary years; but in the opening pages he sketches in briefly his birth and parentage, and the scenes and major events of his childhood; and from these first passages we get hints of carelessness, of temperamental eccentricities and difficulties in the boy which were to disappear from the worldly, balanced record of the man—'I was now . . . put to nurse to one Peter, a neighbour's wife and

tenant, of a good, comely, brown, wholesome complexion, and in a most
sweet place towards the hills, flanked with wood and refreshed with streams;
the affection to which kind of solitude I sucked in with my very milk.'
True, in part ; and becoming a great gardener and horticulturist, he
remained always attracted to the more civilised beauties of rural life, and
even protested sometimes his yearning for 'recess,' as in a letter to Cowley :
'. . . . should think myself more happy than crowned heads were I, as
you, the arbiter of mine own life, and could break from those gilded toys . . .'
But no man has ever been more than Evelyn the arbiter of his own life,
and all his writings calmly set out his polite but obstinate pre-occupation
with the 'gilded toys.'

As a schoolboy, he begged off Eton, being 'unreasonably terrified with
the report of the severe discipline there,' and was schooled, very indiffer-
ently, in Wotton village and at Lewes, taking 'so extraordinary a fancy to
drawing and designing that I could never after wean my inclinations from
it, to the expense of much precious time . . .' At Oxford he seems, by
his own account, to have wasted his time, save that he 'began to look
upon the rudiments of music, in which I afterwards arrived to some formal
knowledge' ; and in the Middle Temple he was plainly bored with the
law, 'that impolished study.' So that when, in his 21st year, he lost his
father, he felt a great anxiety and chill in bereavement, and described
himself as being at that time 'of a raw, vain, uncertain and very unwary
inclination . . . who now thought of nothing but the pursuit of vanity,
and the confused imaginations of young men.'

Such he was then, in the year of his own majority and of the beginning
of Charles the First's bitter struggle against Parliament. When we place
these simple and interesting admissions beside what we know of his
unusual natural talents, the quickness and ease of his mind, the diversity

JOHN EVELYN, 1620-1706
Engraving by Swaine

and excellence of his interests, and when we add that he was rich, free, well-born and honourable, it can be agreed that he was a young man of immense potentialities. Anything might come of the alliance of so many positive endowments with the temperamental diffidences, vanities, curiosities and 'confused imaginations' to which their possessor has confessed. We recall, when we survey the brilliant, dangerous sum of this young man, William Windham, of whose intermittent diary-keeping we shall have occasion to speak later on. But Windham, always conscious of frustration and of the seeds of failure in himself, would have understood, in application to his own soul, Shelley's line about 'the contagion of the world's slow stain'; whereas Evelyn so conditioned and governed himself that it is probable that the relation of such a phrase to his bright and safe maturing would have struck him as sheer nonsense.

Yet the contagion of the world, of his own concern for the world and for having the best of it, did somehow blight his life, making it neatly perfect, like the gardens he cherished, instead of free and incalculable, as it could have been. He took a curious decision in 1642-43—curious,

13

that is, for the man who two hundred years later was to be celebrated in *John Inglesant* as the flower of the Cavalier type. Here it is, in his own words : 'The 12th November was the Battle of Brentford, surprisingly fought ; and to the great consternation of the City, had his Majesty (as it was believed he would) pursued his advantage. I came in with my horse and arms just at the retreat ; but was not permitted to stay longer than the 15th, by reason of the army marching to Gloucester ; which would have left both me and my brothers exposed to ruin, without any advantage to his Majesty. . . . on the 10th (December) returned to Wotton, nobody knowing of my having been in his Majesty's army . . . 12th July, I sent my black menage horse and furniture with a friend to his Majesty, at Oxford. 23rd, The Covenant being pressed, I absented myself ; but, finding it impossible to evade the doing very unhandsome things . . . October the 2nd I obtained a license of his Majesty, dated at Oxford and signed by the King, to travel again.' Thus in November 1643, aged twenty-three and unencumbered, he left England, and stayed away for four years. He returned, a newly married man, but leaving his wife in Paris, in September 1647, 'to settle my affairs' ; stayed for eighteen months, settled into Sayes Court in Deptford, bought and sold manors and works of art, sat for his portrait, studied chemistry, and kept his ear well to the ground in the political scene. 'I got privately into the council of the rebel army at Whitehalle, where I heard horrid villainies.' 'The villainy of the rebels proceeding now so far as to try, condemn and murder our excellent King . . . struck me with such horror that I kept the day of his martyrdom a fast, and would not be present at that execrable wickedness . . .' Six months after the King's execution Evelyn rejoined his wife in Paris, and except for one brief trip home in 1650, stayed abroad until the spring of 1652. He then settled at Deptford, and arranged for his wife to come to England, being advised by his friends 'to compound with the soldiers.' Whence may be said to have begun the full flow of that settled, correct, domestic, scholarly, social and altogether perfect life, which was to run without heat or quarrel and with scarcely a sorrow, scarcely an anxiety, into the beginning of the reign of Anne.

He had decided, at twenty-three, on caution, and on attending to his own interests. Not, so far as we can discover, out of intellectual contempt for the mess his country was in, and not out of lack of interest in the general situation—but simply for selfish reasons. Perhaps he was right. In any case, his decision served him well, and no one ever sought to penalise his curious tepidity. 'He must have conducted himself with uncommon prudence, and address,' writes his first editor, William Bray, in 1818, 'for he had personal friends in the Court of Cromwell at the same time that he was corresponding with his father-in-law, Sir Richard Browne, the ambassador of King Charles II at Paris . . . His manners we may presume to have been most agreeable ; for his company was sought by the greatest

SAMUEL PEPYS, 1632-1703
Oil painting by John Hayls, 1664

men . . . He was happy in a wife of congenial disposition with his own, of an enlightened mind . . . though he remained a decided Royalist, he managed so well as to have intimate friends even amongst those nearly connected with Cromwell; and to this we may attribute his being able to avoid taking the Covenant, which he says he never did take . . .'

Tolerance and tact are excellent things, but it is impossible not to regret the excess of them which we find in Evelyn, and their alliance to self-interest; for passion, that warmth in a man which, even in his mistakes, may make him the friend of his fellowmen and a part of their humanity, could have been nobly mettled by all the gifts which Evelyn preferred to harness to decorum and to social ease. He might have been a leader of his age; he was instead one of its most fixed and untarnished decorations. He wrote a great deal, on politics, on Jesuitism, on the Navy, on Sculpture, on Engraving, on Forestry, Agriculture, and Horticulture.

15

He was linguist, scientist, and amateur of the arts. He helped to found the Royal Society ; and after the Restoration he sat on various Royal Commissions. In all these undertakings he excelled, as also in his duties as husband, father and landowner ; and he lived and died a devout, untroubled Christian. All this, and very much more, we learn from his vast diary, which is an incomparably informative, full picture of a society and an era. It gives us everything that the observant Evelyn saw and touched upon in eighty-five years—except the passions, the urgencies, the doubts, despairs and sins of men, or of one man. The external symptoms of these elements may be touched upon, but only to be banked down by conventional pieties or—when for instance he describes the Fire of London, so admirably, so vividly—with a detachment that is just a shade too cold, too touched with carefulness. '. . . blessing and adoring the distinguishing mercy of God to me and mine, who, in the midst of all this ruin, was like Lot, in my little zoar, safe and sound.' 'Still, the plague continuing in our parish, I could not, without danger, adventure to our church.' 'This night was acted my Lord Broghill's tragedy, called *Mustapha*, before their Majesties at Court, at which I was present . . . I was invited by my Lord Chamberlain . . . though in my mind I did not approve of any such pastime in a time of such judgments and calamities.'

He was too great a man to be so priggish and careful ; too intellectually gifted to hunt so consistently with the hares while he ran with the hounds. But he has left us a splendid panorama, crowded but clear, of a time in English history which was packed with events, with troubles and with development. As a man, measured by his own powers and opportunities, he is disappointing ; but as a diarist he is invaluable.

His friend, Samuel Pepys, a distinguished public servant, kept a diary too—though only for nine years, instead of sixty-five ; and this diary which, it seems clear enough, was never intended for any other eyes besides its writer's, has become the most famous in the world. Everyone knows about it, and most people have read it, or read in it. Pepys began to keep it on 1st Jan., 1660, when he was twenty-seven years old, and just about to be appointed a Clerk of the Acts in the Navy Office ; he was a married man, having in 1655 espoused a young lady of Huguenot extraction ; he was of gentle birth and had been educated at St Paul's and at Cambridge; he was industrious, lively, talented, and had influential friends ; his major desires were to get on in life, to do his work dutifully, and to enjoy himself. Trouble with his eyes compelled him to abandon his diary at the end of May, 1669. He died in 1703, at the age of seventy. In the course of his public life he was Clerk of the Privy Seal, Secretary to the Admiralty, Member of Parliament, President of the Royal Society and Master of Trinity House. Once, because of his loyalty to his chief, the Duke of York, he was charged with implication in the Papist Plot, and sent to prison. He was the friend of Dryden, of Evelyn and of many distinguished

NANCY WOODFORDE
Chalk drawing by Samuel Woodforde

IN THE LAKES

Water colour by J. Varley, 1778-1842

persons. He was interested in literature and in the theatre ; particularly he was interested in music, and was generous and kind to musicians. He liked to dress well, to eat well and to be in on the talk of the town; he liked to dally with women, and to live contentedly with his wife, to control her extravagances, and to see her pretty and happy. He worried about money; he took an interest in his house and its decoration; he collected a library, gave musical parties and was sociable ; he fussed about his health, and every 26th March he piously celebrated his having been successfully 'cut for the stone' on that day in 1658 ; he worked very hard and was trustworthy and scrupulous, staying at his post in London, for instance, all through the panic of the Great Plague. He was, in short, the type, the prototype of the English higher Civil Servant—and he appears to have succeeded better than many such in gratifying his natural ambitions, public and private.

The Diary proves and supports the external story. It does so by the paradoxical method of turning it upside down, or inside out and revealing to us that the basic man on whom this other, this watchful, educated, diplomatic, honest, anxious keeper-up of appearances, is founded is in fact that other's antithesis—naïve, ignorant, reckless, shy, a taker of the silliest risks, a bewildered victim of himself, the creature of his petty impulses, a man forever in danger from his own instabilities and inconsistencies. What could be more interesting, consoling or alarming for any of us to read ? Who is there who has not shuddered to imagine some sudden impossible revelation to the world of his actual self—not the self of this very high or that inexpressibly low moment, but the true small self that frets and chugs along relentlessly, in time with our outward gestures and grimaces ? The self *we* know, but which, while we alternately inflate and enjoy it, or miserably writhe against its monstrous embrace, we are at least determined no one else shall come within miles of knowing ? Pepys has, as nearly as any man ever, brought off this dreadful, unnatural feat—of presenting his whole self, stark naked, quite defenceless, to his fellowmen. No wonder he is an immortal. He has done it very well too—working his whole self, all he is, all his most pitiful and true *minutiae*, into a bright, close, restless picture of London and Court Society during a time that was unusually vivid and loose, unusually dangerous, exciting and worth observation. The story he tells is packed with characters and stories, overflowing with plums for historian and gossip—but he is his own central theme, and he does not mislay himself. Naïve, chattering, and childishly fussed to catch in everything, he gives us, as we say, the works. '. . . My mind, God forgive me, too much running upon what I can *ferais avec la femme de Bagwell demain* . . .' So on, so on ; Krupp and Pierce and Mercer and The. Turner and poor Deb; and all the small sins, ailments and sensations of the common day ; all the humiliations of our wretched, silly flesh. 'Here I did *ce que je voudrais avec* her most freely, and it having cost me 2s. in wine and cake upon her, I away sick of her impudence, and by coach to my Lord Brunker's.' It is an astonishing and, in the full and serious meaning of the word, a shocking achievement.

Perhaps it is somewhat *too* shocking. For my own part, I have never liked Pepys' diary; I have found that a very little of it goes a mighty long way, and at that leaves me bored. To have dared so much for so tiny a result; to empty out breast, brain and entrails, and have so wretchedly little to show for the awful violence; to be, after all and with all said, nothing better or worse than fussy, kindly, nervous, lecherous, dirty, self-pitying and respectable! To be in fact inside, after all the drama of confession, exactly what the outside advertised—no more and no less! That is Pepys—as no doubt it is all of us. And if so, there is the strength and merit of his diary. Yet one must be forgiven for not liking it. It is amusing, but not amusing enough; it is honest, but too pedestrianly; it is realistic, but on themes which are too tiny and too recurrent. It bears about it an *insect* quality; it fidgets the nerves and conscience to no purpose. And it is, for all its pieties, devoid of spiritual pain. It is without light and it is somehow ignoble. In fact I might easily call it a very depressing work. But history and the world are against me—and it is the most famous, the most read and perhaps the best loved of all known diaries.

It is curious that these two most famous of all English diaries remained unpublished until more than a century after the deaths of their authors, and then appeared within seven years of each other: Evelyn's—by permission of the Evelyn family, and edited by William Bray—in 1818; Pepys' in 1825 under the editorship of Lord Braybrooke. Pepys had indeed taken careful measures against easy publication. He wrote his diary in a mixture of shorthand—Shelton's system—and a misleading confusion of foreign words and invented jargon. The manuscript was among his books, which he bequeathed to Magdalene College, Cambridge—and English literature owes one of its most curious and famous possessions to the extraordinarily patient research of an undergraduate of Cambridge called John Smith, who deciphered the text between 1819 and 1822. When it was published in 1825 it naturally caused a vast sensation—and, like Evelyn's Diary, threw floods of light upon seventeenth century society.

Men of the world, Evelyn and Pepys; and their records, though decently strewn with Christian sentiments, portray a society of worldlings, of men and women committed to personal pleasure and personal success. But parallel with their long, complacent lives lived in the glittering capital ran another—spent at first in English villages and country towns, and later either in prisons or on long, difficult journeys in Holland and Germany, in America and the West Indies; and not 'steeple-counting,' as Evelyn might have said, but in pursuit of souls, in spread of grace. George Fox, a weaver's son and the first of the Quakers, was born in Leicestershire in

1624, and died in London in 1681. His *Great Journal* is little read now, I imagine—save by members of the faith he founded; and indeed for the uninitiated layman it makes uneasy, unattractive reading. It is crude, naïve and often turgid; it repeats and overstresses, and labours with too pugnacious simplicity experiences and trains of mystical thought which cannot be conveyed by so much positiveness. But it is impossible to open it anywhere and read a page or two without feeling the pure force of the man behind it, the spiritual generosity, the sheer missionary good-will. It is the textbook of a life dominated by zeal for the good, and by natural understanding of goodness; it is the record of one who quite simply *applied* mysticism to daily life and was perfectly content to suffer for this peculiarity, and to go on preaching its necessity in all times and places, to his last breath. The Journal is an important spiritual work not because it possesses any high literary merit, but because it is passionately sincere and generous, and is the first record of the humble, difficult and often desperate beginnings of a faith which was to become a great social force, and one of the brightest, steadiest lamps which religion has ever lighted upon earth.

OAK TREES UNDER WHICH GEORGE FOX PREACHED THE GOSPEL
View of Flushing, Long Island, North America
Lithograph by Motte after Milbert

THE REVEREND JAMES WOODFORDE, 1740-1803
Oil painting by Samuel Woodforde

No collector of English diaries can escape the Woodforde family. It is probable that between 1600 and 1820 there can hardly have been a day on which one Woodforde or another did not note down what he ate for dinner or what the weather was like, or that the harvest was carried, or that the tailor overcharged him for mending a waistcoat. They were a respectable Northamptonshire and Somerset family of parsons, soldiers, sailors and country gentlemen—and almost all had the diary-hobby, even that one of them, the second or third Samuel Woodforde who stepped so far out of their tradition as to become a painter, and an R.A. In 1932 a twentieth-century member of the family, Miss Dorothy Heighes Wood-forde, published a volume of extracts from what appears to be a great mass of journals—which indicates that between them the Woodfordes have assembled an enormously full and detailed record of English country life over a period of about two hundred and fifty years. It seems that the diaries of Samuel the Academician are merely dull notes of commissions undertaken and people met—and I gather from references to him in Farington's Diaries that he was a dry stick of a man, of no particular charm or talent ; but such pages as I have read from certain other Members of the family have got a kind of slow, comfortable reality in them, and a gentle, unexacting variation of colour and theme, suggestive of English landscape, and carrying the conservative, traditional, place-bound quality, and if you like, charm of English country-house life. Menus, recipes, small scandals, small journeys ; exchange of neighbourly courtesies and acrimonies ; little kindnesses, little tasks ; an earache, an inoculation ; the text of a sermon, a 'scene' of some kind in church ; sixpence won at cards, or a maidservant's dismissal ; a snowstorm, a ripening of cucumbers, a rumour from the wars in France ; the garden, the weather, the walk before dinner—always these three—the garden, the weather . . . it is England that they give us, the Woodfordes ; one particular England, the one they knew and counted on and took for granted as their especial right and pleasure always. And they wrote it down, Nancy, Robert, Samuel, James, with that careful literalness, that adherence to presented facts and unconsciousness of lurking ideas, which has always been the staple of conversation in houses such as theirs ; they give us English country-house life, its very accent and idiom, exactly as the English upper class has evolved and cherished it.

And one Woodforde took the family's hobby a very long way, and made it famous in his own person. The Reverend James Woodforde, born in Somerset in 1740, and Rector of Weston Longeville in Norfolk from 1776 to 1803, the year of his death, began his diary when he was eighteen and kept it up faithfully for the remaining forty-five years of his natural span. *The Diary of A Country Parson*, published in five volumes by the Oxford University Press, became celebrated at its first bow, and is nowadays known and loved by very many readers. 'Reading the Diary of the Reverend James Woodforde is like embarking on a long voyage down a very tranquil stream,' says his editor, Mr J. B. Beresford. 'There is no grand or exciting scenery ; there are no rapids, *nor is there any ultimate expectation of the sea.*' The italics are mine. The five volumes are quite unbeatably non-expectant ; they present as steadily as possible the obvious comings and goings, worries, kindnesses and duties, family and social obligations and pleasures of a typical unpretentious and respectable parson. Nothing more ; but all is set down with a faithful intimacy, and with that repetitiveness which is unavoidable in so close and long a record— so that reading of life in the Weston parsonage—first with troublesome nephew Bill for second string, and later with diary-keeping niece Nancy —becomes after a volume or so the same thing as living there. And it is not altogether dull. There are touches of scandal and fuss ; there are parties—an astonishingly catastrophic one on September 16th, 1777 ; there is a great deal of food and drink ; there are the excitements of the rhubarb purge : 'Sister Clarke, Nancy, Sam and myself all took it into our heads to take a good dose of Rhubarb going to bed . . .' ; and there are outbreaks of horseplay. 'Mrs Davie and Nancy made me up an Apple Pye Bed last night.' 'I took Mrs Davie's garter to-night and kept it. I gave her my pair of garters and I am to have her other to-morrow.' The parson was over forty at this time. 'There are green fields on either side,' says Mr Beresford, in further description of this diary, 'and trees, and a very pleasant murmuring of water . . .' True enough. It catches all the quiet of its place ; it is a benevolent, placid record of habits and customs, unruffled by any hint of mind, or of a private life in the breast.

The Reverend William Cole, of Blechely, Waterbeach and Milton Parsonages, was less suave of temperament than Mr Woodforde ; indeed malicious, contentious, eccentric and with a fair span of tastes and interests —as might be expected of a friend and correspondent of Horace Walpole. His life ran from 1714 to 1782 ; but his diaries, as they have been given to us by Constable, edited by Mr F. G. Stokes and introduced by Miss Helen Waddell, cover only the years 1765 to 1770, when he was in his earlier fifties. The first of these diaries deals with a sojourn in Paris in 1765, whilst Walpole was living there ; the remainder are of country parsonage life, and thick with detail of characters, happenings and humours —to say nothing of details of farm and garden, of food and drink, of health, domestic managements and the expenditure of money. All sharply seasoned with the Reverend William's authoritativeness, guile and acrimony, as well as some pungent reflections on Church and general affairs. He was a meticulous, fussy bachelor, very domesticated and with individual taste. He packs his journals with all these interests, and although the details are wearisome, and there are too many names, too many small disputes, too many capital letters, and too much eccentricity in his prose style, for some tastes—he is undoubtedly an oddity, and has left himself and his scene alive and rich and contributory behind him, for the occasional pleasure of the curious and the nostalgic.

And while the unhurried lives of these divines plodded forward— 'wrote . . . to send a porter to Mr Walpole's for my French china and Pastilles which he bought for me at Paris,' says Mr Cole ; and 'A very comical dull day with us all. Sister Clarke very low. In the evening Sam spoke in favour of the Methodists, rather too much I think,' says Mr Woodforde—Methodism, having long flooded out from Oxford's Holy Club and 'our little society in Fetter Lane,' was sweeping up and down the island, preaching the grace of God without pause or compromise, and indeed by 1770 having established 'The Lord our Righteousness'— newly, formidably, as an uncrushable social force—in Scotland, in Ireland and in New England. John Wesley, born in a Lincolnshire rectory in 1703, had taken Holy Orders and been made a fellow of Lincoln College, Oxford before Rev. James Woodforde was born, and while Mr Cole was

JOHN WESLEY, 1703-1791
Oil painting by Nathaniel Hone, 1766

still at Eton; and as he wasted no time in developing and exercising his missionary vocation, before the latter were middle-aged men the Methodist societies and meetings were a constant part of English life and English news—a controversy, an anxiety, but beyond question a passionate, true force, from which the respect of honest men could not be withheld, and which was impervious to the malignancies of prejudice. And if anyone wonders why a simple, scriptural apostolate, an unblushing appeal to goodness and the sources of grace, could so effectively and rapidly disturb alike the lazy privilege, the sceptic rationalism and the dark, lost ignorance of eighteenth century England, he has only to acquaint himself even a little, by a volume or so of his writing, with John Wesley. And the easiest and truest way to do this is to read a part, or the whole, of his great Journal.

We find there all the chief things that this remarkable man was : the energy, the passion, the organising power, the foresight, the adaptability, the courage and the trenchant, economical eloquence—all of which had share in his missionary success. As a record of sheer, unbroken industry alone it defeats most known biographies, and it paints a very remarkable portrait of a man complicated by a great endowment of attributes—emotional, hard-headed, domineering, intellectual, even sceptical, and brave ; a conservative reformer, a reactionary radical, an arrogant, self-confident saint—all co-ordinated by singleness of purpose, so that a very human man becomes a supernatural force, to transform the lives and hearts of millions.

The story the Journal tells is enormous ; because it is businesslike and thorough and covers the oft-repeated labour of sixty years, it is sometimes dull country for the modern reader, and sometimes, since we cannot, merely by reading of this extraordinary apostolate, find Wesley's 'peace with God,' we can only read in astonished acceptance the scripturally phrased descriptions of conversion. 'Then God began to make bare his arm in an extraordinary manner. Those who were strangers to God felt as it were a sword in their bones, constraining them to roar aloud.' Nor can we feel at ease, at our remove from the fresh impulse, when we read of little children that 'sometimes one, sometimes more, prayed aloud ; sometimes a cry went up from them all, till five or six of them, who were in doubts before, saw the light of God's countenance.' But perhaps we can a little measure what we do not understand or feel at home with in Wesley's Journal by those parts of it that we can apprehend : the honesty, the courage, the mercy and the sheer love of men that bind it together ; the trenchancy of the unaffected prose ; the intelligence of the diarist's comments on his very catholic reading—and, above all, the generous bitterness, the truth, shrewdness and mercy of his observation of life as he finds it : 'Our eyes and ears may convince us there is not a less happy body of men in all England than the country farmers. In general their life is supremely dull, and it is usually unhappy too.' There is plenty of such non-sentimental comment all through the volumes ; highly disturbing to the lazy and the comfortable—as John Wesley compelled his Methodism to be.

Two intellectuals of the eighteenth century wrote diaries which are alike in that each reveals an aspect of its writer's temperament which the rest of his life either concealed or hardly suggests to us. In 1761, when Edward Gibbon was twenty-four and serving as a Captain in the South Hampshire Militia he began a diary, which he kept with fair regularity during three years. The latter part of it, from his arrival in Paris in January 1763 until he reached Rome in May 1764—when it ceased—

VIEW OF PARIS AS GIBBON SAW IT IN 1763
Sepia drawing by Georges Michel

is written in French. It is not a very full, deep or elaborate journal, but it gives an interesting account of his reading and the directions of his thought at a time when he had not yet made up his mind about future work ; also it throws some light on the difficulties placed in the way of a temperament such as Gibbon's—scholarly, ironic, non-combative and of indifferent physical health—by the affectionate interference and domination of an ambitious father, whose only child he was ; and chiefly it is entertaining in that it offers us an unexpected picture—amusing, tolerant and altogether to his credit—of the historian of the Roman Empire in training as a British soldier. As one reads of the scrupulous pains he took with his duties, of how loyally he cared for the prestige and the comfort of his men, of how honestly he gave his attention to the incongruous life—with only a very occasional mild grumble, 'tired of companions who had neither the knowledge of scholars nor the manners of gentlemen'—one is reminded of many young men of his mental colour, who are to-day in like case with Gibbon, though risking much more than he was asked to risk ; not geniuses all, indeed, though one among them may be—but like him impressively gracious and scrupulous in accepting a distasteful occupation and adapting themselves to it. 'I exercised the Battalion for the fourth time, officers and eighteen rounds. These field days were of some service both to men and officers. I am sure they were the greatest to me.' 'We had a field day . . . Tho' I had not exercised them so long yet I found myself very clear and I believe I made no mistakes.' Horace Walpole might lead the wits in scepticism about these volunteers, in a vein which our Home Guard has nowadays learnt to take at its traditional worth : 'John in the rear will be firing his piece into the Backside of his friend Tom in the Front . . .' and the young man, Edward Gibbon, could be humorous too, though more subtly, about his own and his neighbours' soldiering—but while he was at it—mud, route-marches, drinking, noise, regimental disputes and all—he gave it a dutiful, even a genial, attention. And leaving it, summing up the pros and cons of the experience, he says : 'But what I value most is the knowledge it has given me of mankind in general, and of my own country in particular . . . the sum of all is that I am glad the Militia has been, and glad that it is no more.'

William Windham was so versatile, so extravagantly endowed—in birth, possessions, education and friends as well as in personal abilities and graces—that it is surprising to find his career stop short of total success, but perhaps not so surprising that his diaries reveal him as a restless, unhappy man, distrustful of himself, constantly perplexed and at a loss. Yet in his lifetime the world does not seem to have been allowed to know the latter side of the medal ; for when the diaries were published in 1866—more than fifty years after his death—Lord Roseberry observed of them that they dealt 'an almost mortal blow to his reputation.' A comment difficult to understand. Surely when a man has all the gifts, such total absence of smugness as made Windham unhappy and unstable may be allowed to be, though difficult, the ultimate grace ?

He was born in 1750, heir of a distinguished Norfolk name and estate. In youth at Eton and Oxford he excelled in everything, only too easily. In politics he began as a Whig, *protégé* of Fox, and spent a few months in Ireland as Secretary to the Lord Lieutenant in 1783. In 1787 he was, with Burke and Sheridan, a manager of the impeachment of Warren Hastings. At the outbreak of the French Revolution he followed Pitt, and was Secretary for War in 1794, holding office until 1801. He returned to the War Office in 1806, in the 'Ministry of All The Talents.' He died, aged sixty, in 1810. His versatility made friends for him everywhere— among Cabinet Ministers, Oxford dons, actresses, race-horse owners and women of fashion. He read Greek like a scholar, and was exceptionally endowed for mathematical studies ; he loved prize-fights ; he made a perilous ascent in a balloon ; he interested himself in country matters and the business of his estate ; he was a constant student of Shakespeare, and a close friend and critic of Mrs Siddons ; he was devoted to Burke and admired by Fanny Burney ; he loved Dr Johnson with devotion. He was successful with women, and—the diaries make it clear—he found the exactions of sexual love a major cause of restlessness and dissatisfaction. He had love-affairs, but the most constant and uneasy was with Mrs Byng,

WILLIAM WINDHAM, 1750-1810
Oil painting by Sir Joshua Reynolds

wife of the Hon. John Byng, afterwards Viscount Torrington. After many years of restless, uncertain intrigue with her, their feeling resolved into friendship, and late in life he married her younger sister, Cecilia Forrest, who had long been devoted to him. The marriage was childless, and appears to have been happy.

The journals make dry and somewhat tired comment on all the emotions, friendships, ambitions, projects and disappointments of a full life. They are revelatory only of Windham's dissatisfaction with himself, and into that they do not plunge wholeheartedly. They ring wearily for the most part; there is nothing in them to resolve the enigma of his life, or expose its heart—but they do deepen and underline it, adding a grace of sadness and second thoughts to a personal history which might otherwise seem monotonously brilliant.

We will depart from the eighteenth century under the nimble, bright escort of Fanny Burney. She breaks new ground. For one thing, she is

the first English *woman* of any significance—*pace* the Woodforde ladies—
who has left us a diary. For another, she leads us, a little unfairly, towards
a suspicion which later increases somewhat, that women make more re-
freshing, more effective diarists than men. Be that as it may, you may have
your Pepys and Evelyn and, with both hands, the pettifogging parsons—
except Rev. Francis Kilvert—if you will leave me Fanny Burney ; all the
uneven, over-written seventy years of her industrious and spirited jotting-
down.

She was born in 1752 and she died in 1840 ; she began to keep her
diary in 1768, when she was sixteen, and she made her last entry in it on
5th March 1839, when she was eighty-seven. 'I broke off, and an incapable unwillingness seized my pen,' that last note begins—and we feel
the old lady's petulant surprise. Incapable unwillingness had not normally
been her trouble with a pen. Indeed her *Juvenile Journal*, covering the
years before she published *Evelina* and 'Addressed to a Certain Miss
Nobody' is torrentially, excessively facile—and at times too facetious and
coy for present-day taste. But when she romps overmuch, we can remind
ourselves that she is very young, at least during the first four or five
hundred pages, and also that a great deal of the clatter is in fact sheer
talent that has not yet perceived or taken hold of itself. And perhaps
the final impression left with us when we reach 5th March 1839 is that—
for all her success, for all the brilliance and fun and fame, and though
she will always hold a place in English letters—the gifted creature never
measured her own powers, never extended or wrestled with them, and
thus never became the writer she was born to be. Her first success surprised and enchanted her—and she seems to have gone on being surprised,
enchanted and a touch amateurish to the end.

Most people know the outline of her life. She was one of the large
family of Dr Charles Burney, musician and historian of music, and she
spent a free and happy girlhood in London, educating herself at random
and enjoying the brilliant, varied society of her father's friends—musical,
theatrical, intellectual and merely fashionable. She surprised her world,
and her family, with *Evelina* when she was twenty-six, becoming famous
at a blow, and becoming moreover Dr Johnson's 'Fannikin' and his 'little
Burney.' Reynolds, Burke, Windham, Sheridan became her friends ;
Mrs Thrale took her up, and she met Mrs Montague and all the 'Blues' ;
Madame de Genlis sought her out on her first visit to England, and wooed
her friendship ; and the aged Mrs Delaney patronised her—with the
unfortunate result that the foolish Fanny, after having repeated the *Evelina*
success with *Cecilia*, found herself, at the age of thirty-three and when a
famous woman of letters, installed as Second Mistress of the Robes to
Queen Charlotte, the dull wife of George III. 'And now began a slavery
of five years,' says Macaulay, and '. . . we are utterly at a loss to conceive
how any human being could endure such a life, while there remained a

THE GARRICKS ENTERTAINING DR. JOHNSON
Oil painting by Johann Zoffany, 1725-1810

vacant garret in Grub Street, a crossing in want of a sweeper, a parish
workhouse or a parish vault.' Without being quite so extravagantly at a
loss, we marvel too—especially as we read the diarist's brilliantly revelatory
account of life as Queen Charlotte's attendant. It was an absurd appoint-
ment, and it broke Miss Burney's health and she had to be released from
it. Thereafter she fell into the society of some *émigrés* from the French
Revolution and in 1793, at the age of forty-one, she married the penniless
Chevalier d'Arblay and settled down with him in a cottage in Surrey, to
live on her court pension of £100 a year. They had one child, a son,
and they were very happy. The diaries are in nothing better than in their
restrained, true portrayal of her marital peace, and the sweetness and gaiety
with which they recount the baby years of her child, and her delight in
him. From 1801 to 1810 she lived in France, her husband's fortunes
being somewhat restored under Napoleon; she brought her son back to
England in the latter year, and rejoined her husband in France in 1814.
She was in Brussels in 1815, and her diaries contain a famous account of
June of that year, and the thunders and repercussions of Waterloo. There-

after her husband settled in England again, until his death in 1818. Her son, who became a clergyman, died unmarried in 1837. Between her marriage and her death she did much literary work—some unsuccessful plays, a novel, *Camilla*, and an unreadable novel called *The Wanderer*, for which she is said to have received £7,000 ; also *Memoirs of Dr Burney* and some pamphlets—as well as the never neglected diaries.

It is well she did not neglect them, for they are the best of her, and her chief claim on immortality. They are so much better than most diaries because they are imaginative, free and subjective ; they are, in fact, the work of a *writer*, which most diaries are not. Miss Burney does not stick to the facts of each day in the sense of merely setting them down ; she uses them, expands them, enjoys herself with them, and lets us take all those details for granted which she does not select as essential to her vein of narrative. She gives us conversations—with Mrs Thrale, with Windham, with George III, with Talleyrand, or with her little son—not *verbatim* or in any kind of shorthand but as her imagination and her brilliant memory feel them when they echo in her afterwards—so that they are truer than truth and, without strain or apparent falsification, achieve a richness, a certainty of character and a sequence and pace which in fact they almost certainly did not have, but which the artist rightly felt they merited.

As we read, and taste the variety of her experiences and the power, understanding and charm which she brought to bear on all she encountered, we cannot but wonder why she never took herself in hand and became a great novelist, as great as Jane Austen. She seems to have had all the needed natural abilities ; and she had besides a wide knowledge of life and the world, she had the goodwill of all the best minds of her day, she had health and long life and a great zest for writing. Yet she never mastered these advantages and soared to genius on them.

The reason may lie with her benevolent and rather foolish father. Not in any of his conscious acts—for though it clearly was silly of him to persuade her, with Mrs Delaney, into becoming a Mistress of the Robes, we do not go all the way with Macaulay in his shocked tirades against the Doctor for this ill-judged piece of snobbery and worldly hopefulness— for Fanny was, after all, thirty-one then and famous, and had twice resoundingly proved her ability to succeed in letters ; she could have decided for herself against an undertaking which, the diaries make clear, she viewed with uneasy fear. 'I have always and uniformly had a horror of a life of attendance and dependence . . . Could I but save myself from a lasting bond ? ' However, she did not save herself ; and this major occasion is only the full declaration of a curious docility that ran all through her life, often weakening or tarnishing its merits.

I trace this to her father—and not to any fault of his, but to his unconscious, potent influence on her. She loved him very much, and he was in childhood and girlhood the source and inspirer of all that ease and fun

FANNY BURNEY, 1752-1840
Oil painting by E. F. Burney

and pleasant learning and talented go-as-you-please in which she and her
sisters were so happy. The love, the confidence he bred in Fanny would
seem to have trained her into a marked dependence on the elderly, and a

curious need to be loved by them, and to take their directions. She loved her father; and also in girlhood she loved the elderly Mr Samuel Crisp of Chessington, 'Daddy' Crisp, for whom with her sister Susan all the early diaries were written. 'My papa always mentions him by the name of my *Flame*. Indeed he is not mistaken—himself is the only man on earth I prefer to him.' She loved Dr Johnson with veneration for the last years of his life, and sought his company constantly, though she was only in her twenties; she was for a time during Dr Johnson's life the slave of the already elderly Mrs Thrale; she adored the venerable and boring Mrs Delaney; she persuaded herself that she adored the 'sweet Queen' Charlotte, and similarly that she had a great affection for poor George III at his maddest and feeblest; and when at last she loved a man enough to marry him, he too was elderly, in his middle fifties. All these people, from elderly to aged, were at different periods the dominating influences in her life; they advised her, they moulded her, and she seemingly found it impossible ever to doubt their wisdom, be sceptical about them, or give them, however privately, a disrespectful or a rebellious thought. They intimidated her, though she did not perceive it, for she needed, in some obscure way, their elderly authority; she needed, in every important relationship, to find an element of her first strong filial devotion. And all these influences, while they made her happy and flattered her and gave her a sense of safety, not only led her away from her more forceful and self-reliant parts, in which she might have found the true ore of her talent, but also turned her back from adventures in friendship which might have helped her to that end. For constantly in the diaries we are disappointed by fits of prudery and caution which can only have been induced by the shocked gossip of the old, and must have arisen from the docile need to 'please papa' in everything—as when she nonsensically took Dr Johnson's cue and ended her friendship with Mrs Thrale because the latter chose to marry Mr Piozzi; and later in life abandoned in turn her friends Madame de Genlis and Madame de Stael—simply because of *rumours* about their private lives and while protesting her personal sense of loss and her admiration of the ladies' talents. Such parochialism and docility to the views of the cautious sit ill with her wit, her keen interest in character and her general liveliness and *verve*. But they run all through the bright fibre of her life, and seem to spring from that early, first desire to be everything her father most admired. All the rest of life had to be dovetailed into that essential.

'November 11th, Wednesday. Baked bread and giblet pie—put books in order—mended stockings. Put aside dearest C.'s letters, and now at about seven o'clock we are all sitting by a nice fire. Wm. with his book and a candle, and Mary writing to Sara.' It is 1801, we are at Grasmere,

BENJAMIN HAYDON 1786-1846
Pencil and red chalk drawing by G. H. Harlow, 1816

CHELSEA BRIDGE FROM MILLBANK
Water colour by Joseph Farington, 1790

and Dorothy Wordsworth is making her gentle note of the day. And it is hardly necessary for us to interrupt her, or do more than name her here among our English diarists—for the publication in 1941 of all her *Journals*, under the editorship of Mr E. de Selincourt, created such a happy new *réclame* for her and was received with such universal pleasure that she certainly stands in no further need of commendation. And I observe this all the more contentedly since I have to admit—making, so far as I know, a minority of one—that the *Journals* disappoint me taken as a whole, and when considered in relation to the personality we know their writer to have been. All except the *Grasmere Journal* (1800-1803) and the brief *Alfoxden Journal*, which in their kind—though not the kind we might have longed for—are perfect ; and parts of the *Journal Of A Tour In The Isle Of Man* (1828), which in spite of premonitory shadows here and there of sadness and ill-health contains much of the simple, lyrically-touched realism, the fastidious, clear selectiveness which distinguish so especially the Grasmere pages.

But though we could not spare any one of her exquisitely measured strokes of simple observation—'Wytheburn looked very wintry, but yet there was a foxglove blossoming by the roadside—' knowing Dorothy Wordsworth somewhat from the loves and friendships she won and kept—from Coleridge, from the Lambs, from Crabb Robinson, from all her brother's admirers, and from the adored brother himself—we want from her in her writings more of that 'meddling intellect' that William inveighed against ; we want her thoughts as well as her observations, and when she 'walked with Coleridge,' when 'William and I strolled in the wood,' when 'we had a sweet and tender conversation' we desire exasperatedly to know a little at least of what was said. There is too much suppression everywhere in Dorothy Wordsworth of what clearly must have been a most distinguished and original mind ; too much daily practice of that 'wise passiveness' which William invoked, but—we surmise, for all his sister's passionate care of his legend—did not easily command. Curiously, we might think after reading her *Journals* that Dorothy is, by temperament, that ideal poet of the Preface to *Lyrical Ballads* whom William believed himself to be. But she did not write verse, and she undertook to be William's angel—so egoism and intellectual restlessness were subjugated by responsibilty and by love ; and she is so loyal, so discreet that we are never allowed to guess at any possible second thoughts. Her glinting, delicate sense of humour, which she uses sparingly, is never allowed to hurt William or anyone else—although his humourlessness, his quality of seeming to have been born an old man, must often have puzzled, not to say wearied, a companion so girlishly, though fastidiously, willing to be amused. The poet was, when he travelled abroad, prone to make scenes—and though Dorothy records these as justified, she cannot quite keep humourous uneasiness at bay. 'Mary and I walked on ahead . . .' and

'Wm. refused to give more than the sum agreed for—the man grew impertinent—and William desired the Magistrate might be summoned—a woful resource!' Such gleams relieve the repetitive descriptions of scenery which abound in *A Tour Of The Continent* (1820); but there are not enough of them, and there is far too much guide-book observation. Love made her too discreet. No one could wish her to be crudely expansive about, for instance, the trip she took with William to Calais in August 1802, to visit Annette and his daughter Caroline, before his marriage to Mary Hutchinson—but is it unnatural to be surprised that the circumstances induced no greater depth of comment, no closer or more individual reflections than she made on any other of their journeys?

Still, she has left us the small, imperishable beauties of the *Grasmere Journal*, its constant loveliness heightened by sweet, plain touches. '. . . I sate half an hour afraid to pass a cow. The cow looked at me and I looked at the cow, and whenever I stirred the cow gave over eating.' 'The Lake of Rydale calm, Jupiter behind, Jupiter at least *we* call him, but William says we always call the largest star Jupiter.' '. . . at last I eased my heart by weeping—nervous blubbering, says William. It is not so.'

Between 1809 and 1811 an eccentric poor governess lived at a house called Dove's Nest on Windermere. 'There are many characters here worth observation,' she wrote in her diary, or letter-book. 'S. Coleridge, the conductor of a new and valued publication entitled "The Friend," resides only a few miles hence.' But she never mentions the Wordsworths, with whom Coleridge was then living at Allan Bank; and though she occasionally records going to Grasmere church on Sunday she does not seem to have known that a great poet lived so near her. Her employers, the wild and frantic Pedders who led her a terrible dance, would not have been sympathetic to William or to 'dearest C.'—so the remarkable and forthright Miss Weeton, brushing just wide of a chance of mention in Miss Wordsworth's diaries, did well, and rather better, to keep her own.

She was an obscure, unlucky woman, born in Upholland, Lancashire, in 1777, and brought up in great poverty by her widowed mother who kept a little dame school, and handed it on to her daughter. Miss Weeton forged out from it in exasperation in her thirties and became a governess, scraped an independent living one way and another, was trapped by a brother, for his own ends, into a wretched marriage, stormed out of that, fought a long, wild battle for the custody of her one child—won the battle, established herself as a respectable citizen in Wigan, and died feared, and long remembered I should think by all her relatives and connections. The humble but vehement and unusual story was set down by her, year in year out, in vigorous diaries, and in letters which she copied and embodied very carefully in the diaries. These were neglected and ignored by her people after her death, but by chance in the '30s of this century fell into the sympathetic hands of Mr Edward Hall and, edited by him, were published by the

QUEEN VICTORIA'S FIRST PRIVY COUNCIL
Detail showing Greville at the extreme left
Oil painting by Sir David Wilkie, 1785-1841

Oxford University Press in two volumes, in 1936 and 1939. They run
from 1807 to 1825, and give a close, realistic picture of small-town life
in England at that time—while building up with amazing strokes of humour,
coarseness, truth, self-acclamation, pride and intelligence, a full-size por-

trait of a very remarkable female—one who in an easier walk of life, or with even an ounce or two more of education or of luck, might have done remarkable things, or given a lot of trouble, or somehow made herself remembered. Space forbids me to linger with Miss Weeton—I can only commend her in passing to those who like originals, and do not mind being bludgeoned—at a remove of more than a hundred years.

HENRY CRABB ROBINSON, 1775-1867
Drawing after a miniature by Masquerier

In the great world at this period, far from the Lakes and from Up-holland—in Fanny Burney's world—a great many journals were piling up, in secret or in semi-secret. The first half of the nineteenth century saw well to its own documentation. Creevy, Greville, Croker: Joseph Farington, Benjamin Haydon; Lady Blessington, Lady Holland; Moore, Byron, Rogers, Telford, Scott—these and many others consumed a great deal of ink in their day, assembling what were to be their 'papers'—memoirs, reminiscences, letters—not always diaries. Thomas Creevy, for instance, who moved in Prince Regent and Holland House circles, was believed by Greville and others to have kept 'copious diaries,' as to the destiny of which there was some anxiety at his death in 1838. But when his 'papers' were published there was found to be almost no diary—only an occasional passage in that form wedged in among his letters to his wife and to his stepdaughter. These letters are, however, so lively and malicious that one cannot but regret the diaries of which he was suspected, but which perhaps he never wrote.

Charles Greville, who held the post of Clerk to the Council and was intimate with statesmen of all parties, and particularly with the Duke of Wellington and with Palmerston, kept journals from 1818 to 1860, had a wonderful *flair* for the right kind of backstairs news, and has provided posterity with some excellent entertainment. Joseph Farington R.A., an inconsiderable painter, but a man of authority and shrewdness who devoted himself zestfully to Academy affairs, kept a diary from 1793 to the last day of his life, December 30th, 1821. Everyone who is anyone appears in it, and therefore it is a useful reference book for historians or biographers of the period ; but in manner and tone it is dull, and does nothing to attract us to its writer.

A very different kind of man, Benjamin Haydon—resembling Farington only in being a bad painter—also kept a journal, from 1821 to his death, by suicide, in 1846. Haydon was energetic, pugnacious, intelligent, most naïvely conceited and never out of trouble—and his diary reflects him vividly, and is alternately maddening and very entertaining. He has a good narrative manner and plenty of humour, except about himself, a subject on which he could not look unemotionally. He makes good observations on painters : 'Tintoretto has not the solidity of Rubens or Titian ; Titian was full of sensation.' And he reports parties well—the terrible christening party for Hazlitt's child, and an evening when Mrs Siddons read *Macbeth* to a number of gentlemen who were eating toast and drinking tea, they in an agony lest they clatter or crunch. 'Curious to see Lawrence in that predicament, to hear him bite by degrees and then stop for fear of making too much crackle.' Haydon was a friend and correspondent of Keats, of whom he says with absurd complacency: 'Poor, dear Keats. Had Nature but given you firmness as well as fineness of nerve . . .' Yet, years after Keats' death, he writes touchingly : 'I dreamt last night of dear Keats. I thought he appeared to me and said : 'Haydon you promised to make a drawing of my head, . . .' Haydon died in sudden despair, after years blustering for solvency and fame—and he is remembered now not as a painter, not even as the man who fought the Academy in the cause of the Elgin Marbles, but merely as a friend of Keats, and perhaps also because Hazlitt said he was the best talker he ever knew.

But the period of all these journals, indeed the first sixty years of the nineteenth century, have been recorded quite superbly—from the point of view of historians, biographers and gossip-hunters—by a prince of extrovert diarists, Henry Crabb Robinson. What we have in published form of this indefatigable man—reminiscences, letters and diaries—and a very great deal has not been printed—makes an invaluable body of information and eye-witness comment. To try to catalogue Crabb Robinson's famous friends, or his interests, or his travels, or his social activities would be absurd. He had, since he must have been abnormally sociable, a wonderful life. He was of respectable, modest origin, the son of a tanner in Bury St. Edmunds. He spent his youth as an attorney's clerk ; then, inheriting an income of £100 a year, he went to Germany when he was twenty-five, and remained there five years, studying at Jena and Frankfurt, and later meeting in Weimar all the greatest Germans of the century— Goethe, Schiller, Wieland, Herder, Schlegel. Also he met the ubiquitous Madame de Stael, and 'mon Benjamin,' Benjamin Constant. In England, to which he returned in 1805, his earliest friends—but he never seemed to lose a friend or to slacken in the upkeep of friendship—were Hazlitt, the Lambs, Mrs Barbauld, Coleridge, the Wordsworths, the Flaxmans, Blake, Miss Mitford—but eventually every interesting, intelligent or especially gifted person in England was on his list, never to be removed from it. He joined the staff of *The Times* and was its correspondent in Sweden and in Spain in 1807-1808. From 1813 to 1838 he practised at the Bar and having made enough money with which to be solvent and generous for the rest of his days he retired, to give himself up to a variety of good works and pleasant pursuits.

He was not a brilliant man ; but he had a sound understanding, was industrious, loyal and balanced, and he must have had a genius for friendship. His diaries are innocent of malice, but they are not at all fatuous. His sturdy devotion to Coleridge through thick and thin, his unflurried interest in Blake, and his wise, calm passion—if passion *can* be thus qualified—for Goethe prove capacity of mind and an appetite for the difficult. And the value for us of his devotion to genius is the simplicity, unaffected and pure of sycophancy, with which he writes down his impressions. When he notes some of Blake's difficult aphorisms : 'I regret that I have been unable to do more than put down these few things,' he says. 'The tone and manner are incommunicable. There are a natural sweetness and gentility about Blake which are delightful.'

The modest diarist might have been surprised to learn that *his* readers in their turn would find, all through his laborious contributions to posterity another kind of 'natural sweetness and gentility . . . which are delightful.'

Crabb Robinson does not appear to have known Caroline Fox, although many of his friends were also hers, and he would have sympathised with her intellectual interests and with her spiritual idiom. She kept a diary, from 1835, when she was sixteen, to her death in 1871. She was born and always made her home in Cornwall. Her father was Robert Were Fox, Quaker, distinguished geologist and F.R.S. Caroline, who never married, was herself a devout Quaker, and of intellectual and austere tastes—though warm and humorous too, very quick and appreciative with life and people. Chief among her famous friends were John Stuart Mill, John Sterling and the Carlyles. She regularly paid long visits to London,

CAROLINE FOX, 1819-1871
Etching by Hubert Herkomer

and went abroad with her father on his travels and, towards the end of her life, in search of health. Her *Journal*, though in fact a touch too impersonal for all its air of ease and intimacy, is a very intelligent record of the observations and moods of many great and distinguished people ; there are attractive notes on the diarist's own reading, and there is a sense of sweetness and natural holiness throughout. Good anecdotes too : Jane Welsh Carlyle reporting of Geraldine Dewsbury that she 'declares herself born without any sense of decency ; the publishers beg that she will be decent, and she has not the slightest objection to be so, but she does not know what it is.' Sir Henry de la Beche and Warrington Smith being unnerved at a dinner party by the young Florence Nightingale, who led them *via* geology 'into regions of Latin and Greek' and Egyptian inscriptions. 'But when she began quoting Lepidus . . . "A capital young lady that, if she hadn't so floored me with her Latin and Greek ! " ' Tennyson, in 1860: '. . . but when he heard the name of Hallam, how his great grey eyes opened, and gave one a momentary glimpse of the depths in which *In Memoriam* learnt its infinite wail.'

In 1938, '39, '40 there appeared for the first time in print—published by Jonathan Cape—three volumes entitled *Kilvert's Diary*. Mr William Plomer was their editor. He had found a prize indeed—and the prize fell luckily into discreet and sympathetic hands. Anything might have happened to Francis Kilvert when being dressed for presentation to the reading public of the past twenty years, for he lays his soul right open to the mockery, the cleverness or the portentous psycho-analytical wisdom of our time. Mr Plomer, however, was content to read and enjoy him, assemble all available facts and associations, and present the diarist to us with only the necessary amount of just and friendly comment.

Francis Kilvert was born in a Somerset rectory in 1840. He went to Oxford and took Holy Orders. After a period assisting his father, who was then rector of Langley Burrell in Wiltshire, he went as curate to Clyro in Breconshire, where he worked for seven years. Afterwards he had a living at St. Harmon's in Radnorshire, and finally that of Bredwardine in Herefordshire. He married when he was thirty-eight, and five weeks after his marriage he died very suddenly of peritonitis. His published diary runs, with breaks, from 1870 to the spring of the year in which he died, 1879.

Its most obvious merit is the clear and detailed picture it gives us of life in the English countryside seventy years ago. Kilvert gets it all in, and makes it much more vivid and worth reading about than do the eighteenth century parsons, because he has enthusiasm for living, takes pains, has an unusually eager, bright eye, and—being very sentimental—gets all external things related to himself. He gives us, like a painter, not the flat actuality but his own composition of it. He gives us all the 'properties' of his kind of life indeed, all the things we know that are almost 'stock' now, and that we have encountered over and over again in period novels and family albums, but he gives them *as he feels them*, and as partaking of his vitality: walks, sermons, frosty mornings, visits to parishioners; toothache, confirmation caps, talk of the Franco-Prussian War, 'a letter from my mother'; girls and kisses and 'mischievous, saucy glances from beautiful grey eyes'—a very great deal about girls and glances; croquet parties, chubby babies, news from India, the funeral of an eccentric aunt (this last being quite superbly done); archery, dances, kisses—'ten miles for a kiss'; prayers by the bedsides of dying children; a great deal of scenery; visits to Oxford; pious reflections, and sudden 'romps' (undefined)—'a screaming romp with Lucretia who in rolling about upon the bed upset the candle on the coverlet and burst into peals of inextinguishable laughter . . .'; talks with Mr Barton, 'a clever, well-read man,' about the Holy Grail; 'sun on the lawn . . . claret cup iced . . . after dinner we had archery.' It might be dull, it might grow tiresome—even though on plain, objective merits many passages are lovely—crystal clear and complete. 'Chippenham bells pealing and firing all day for the Queen's

QUEEN VICTORIA AT OSBORNE, 1865
Oil painting by Sir Edwin Landseer

MOUNT EREBUS FROM HUT POINT

Water colour by Dr. E. A. Wilson drawn on the Second Scott Expedition, 1911-1913

birthday. Perch fished while I lay on the sloping bank and read *The Spanish Student*. The river was very low and the roach and dace have not yet come up. The air was full of "green drake" or mayfly just come up and all swarming over the river, and the little bleak leaping at them every moment.' Or this—a different statement, quite as clear and complete : 'Just as I heard the breakfast bell ring across the Common from the Rectory and turned in at the black gate a man crossed the stile carrying a basket. He said his name was Summerflower, that he had fasted since yesterday morning and that he could buy no breakfast before he had got watercresses to sell.' Yet such things, though they need not be any better done, would not in themselves bestow its curious originality and freshness on this diary. Nor would it be truthful to say that Kilvert always describes as well as in these passages. 'Considered simply as a writer of prose he shows a decided talent,' says Mr Plomer. Agreed ; but it is talent only—that is, talent undeveloped, unconsidered by its owner, and therefore too frequently unbridled. I am willing to be indulgent, with his editor, to his 'copious flow of adjectives'—but not for their own sakes, and not for the prose they give us when they are let loose, but because they are an unavoidable part of Francis Kilvert, they express him, for better or worse, in terms of his period and of himself—and so must be accepted with the rest of this remarkable self-portrait. But I do not think that he was more than a potential writer of good prose—for it always seems to have been hit or miss; an atmosphere, a memory, a mood could control him and make him write as it dictated ; but *he* could not control those masters—which only means that he never *learnt* to write, but simply wrote ; in the most alarming, rich gushes, if that was how he felt—*vide* the entry 'From My Bedroom Window' for July 11th, 1870—or gently, objectively or humourously, when such states ruled him. I do not believe that he considered his writing at all, save with the pleasure of a boy in doing something which everyone could not do. And in the period in which he lived, with its influences of eloquence, colour, tears and tenderness, that was not a safe way to be a prose writer. Not that there is any safety—artistic or emotional—in Francis Kilvert ; I think indeed that he got through so decently, as man and as writer, simply by the grace of God and the luck of the innocent.

Sometimes, taking his prose at its wildest, he reminds one of all our great-aunts, and of the poems and letters which they used to write when an infant died in the family, or had a birthday. 'Then the girls would have me go into the next room to see Janet in bed. So we went in and found her pretty and rosy with tumbled curly hair lying in her little soft white nest contentedly sucking chocolates. I sat down upon her bed and the rest gathered and so Queen Janet held her court as pleased as possible... soon had her round plump limbs out from under the sheets with the innocent simplicity of childhood and her pretty little feet in my lap . . .

rosy and curly and still contentedly sucking her chocolate. Dear Ruthie stood by her little sister, kind, sweet and motherly. They share their little bed together, "two dumplings" as Ruthie said . . . Then the father dressed for dinner came in to see his children and to wish them Good-night. It was a lovely family group, a beautiful picture.' Or read him as he muses over a silk bookmarker with 'Forget-Me-Not' embroidered on it—'the short, simple prayer.' 'It was a gift from a child sweetheart. But from which? I gazed at the words conscience-stricken. Forget-me-not. And I had forgotten . . . The whole scene rose before me, the old cottage fireside at evening and the fair head and pure eyes of a child bent earnestly over her work, and the little hands eager about her labour of love . . . "Forget Me Not. I will send it to-morrow and he will not forget." And I have forgotten. The vision faded. Oh, the fickleness and forgetfulness of man and the faithfulness of woman. Alas, it is the old story . . .' It is a shame to have to chop up such a passage, but Kilvert is not economical when he dreams. And I do not quote it so much *pour rire* as to show that he wrote without judgment, though in a sense with an abundance of talent.

It is the unevenness, the eccentricity and the sheer naturalness of the writer which distinguish this diary. Kilvert puts down everything and anything, a landscape, a joke, a prayer, or a rhapsody about yet another girl; and, whatever it is, he lights it up; by some curious trick of his vitality and his innocence, he makes everything *live* that he touches.

Except perhaps girls. Because girls render him helpless. Any girl, from two years old to twenty-five, in her perambulator or at the churn or in Sunday school or being a bridesmaid or playing croquet or castrating a lamb or lying on her deathbed—any girl sets him off; about her sweet blue eyes and bright sweet morning face and rounded arms as creamy as the milk and her tossing curls and teasing glance and half-veiled charms. Girls, from their cradles to their wedding beds, moved him so much that he quite simply was unable to see them for emotion, and can be said to have been girl-blind. For it is impossible that Wiltshire, Radnorshire and Breconshire could have contained such an extraordinary number of shattering, innocent, merry beauties in that one decade seventy years ago. It is just that they were girls. 'O my child if you did but know!' and 'Ah Gipsy!' and 'Angels ever bright and fair' and 'Farewell, farewell!' and 'I thought—was it so?—that there were tears in those blue eyes when we parted.' No reader could keep track of the journey of this clergyman's heart—for apart from official wooings, of 'sweet Daisy Thomas,' of 'Kathleen Mavourneen' or of 'bewitching Etty Brown,' he records very, very many other strongly protested loves. 'Lovely Florence Hill' and the 'Gipsy Child' and his 'mountain maid,' and the girls he 'romped' with, and the girls he longed to know better, and the little girls at Sunday school, and the girls he visited in sickness, and the girls he buried.

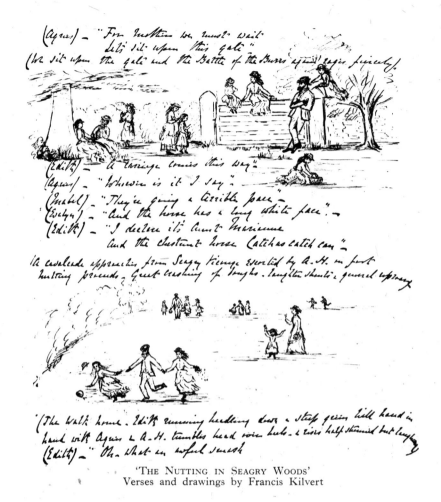

'THE NUTTING IN SEAGRY WOODS'
Verses and drawings by Francis Kilvert

Parallel with this ever-rushing emotionalism runs a good rough stream of coarseness, of plain sensuality in thought, and of shameless enjoyment of the beating of children. Yet he was kind—and good. He was limited indeed by his own *naïveté* and his acceptance of outward forms, and by the characteristics, some of the worst characteristics, of his age. But he was loved in his parishes; he knew his people well, frequented them, helped them, grieved with them and 'romped' with them. He preached the Christianity of his time, and clearly he did his best to live as a Christian. He worked tirelessly and without self-pity, and in little things he was kind. If he met an old woman carrying buckets of water he carried them for her; he carried his musical box up a considerable mountain climb 'for the blind child'; in his way he understood children and made good jokes about

43

them, and noted what they said with an unusually selective ear. And he really loved the beautiful country about him, its ancientry and simplicity, and its seasonal changes and occupations. He seems to have been a happy man on the whole in spite of his sensitivity ; he had an outgoing, generous temperament, and great consideration (despite the flogging complex) for the feelings of others ; he was tolerant, and touchingly easy to please. 'The morning was perfectly glorious, a brilliant cloudless blue sky . . . and the gossamers shone and twinkled into green and gold in the grass which in the shade of the wood was still hoary with the night's frost . . . After luncheon I played croquet with the girls.'

And now we will leave all this Victorianism with a salute to its Queen, who also was a diarist. Many people have read the excerpts of her diaries which are published with her letters, and many more, of the older generations, are familiar with the once very popular *Leaves From The Journal Of Our Life In The Highlands*. By reason of her place and greatness any writings of Queen Victoria must have interest, and some have found much to admire, or even to charm them, in the closer revelation of her personality which the diaries give. Some, on the other hand, have not, and remain unattracted by the dauntless, arrogant, obstinate little old lady. But certainly the Highland Diary is good fun, for us who can view those perpetual, freezing expeditions and picnics in the rain at our very safe remove. And Francis Kilvert, at least, would have admired the Queen's extraordinary prose, and shared her enthusiasm for scenery—and even perhaps for lunching 'on a cairn of stones, in a piercing cold wind.' For he was polite and adaptable in a way we have forgotten, and certainly he was a most loyal subject of Her Majesty.

So far the twentieth century, pre-war, war and post-war periods has shown no sign of dropping the well-established diary habit. And now war again—we assuredly have plenty to record for those who come after. It is as well, I suppose, that the diarists should persevere. But out of the stream already published, from Sir Algernon West and Wilfrid Scawen Blunt, by way of Colonel Repington, Sir Henry Wilson and Arnold Bennett down to Ego 1, 2, 3, 4 and 5, I choose here to make reminder of only three diaries—and those reminders shall be brief. All three were written under exceptional stress and ordeal, and bear little spiritual relation to traditional English diaries—therefore they seem particularly representative of our time.

The last diary of Captain Scott is good to read now, for morale's sake, as a reminder of the power of courage, and of the dignity of men. Everyone knows the magnificent story of his last journey to the South Pole, and whoever knows the story knows the diary, which was found in the tent on the Barrier with the three dead men. The entries of the last two months are immortal. 'Wednesday January 17.—The Pole. Yes, but under very different circumstances. We have had a horrible day . . . Now for the run home and a desperate struggle. I wonder if we can do it.' 'Jan. 24th. . . . I don't like the easy way Oates and Evans get frost-bitten.' 'Feb. 8th. A lot could be written on the delight of setting foot on rock after 14 weeks of snow and ice . . . It is like going ashore after a sea voyage.' 'Feb. 24th. It is great luck having the horsemeat to add to our ration . . .' 'Feb. 29th. Every day we have been ready to start for our depot 11 miles away but outside the door of the tent it remains a scene of whirling drift . . . we are getting weaker, of course, and the end cannot be far. It seems a pity, but I do not think I can write more. R. Scott. For God's sake look after our people.'

That was the end of one of the greatest of all stories, which can be read at any time with benefit ; and now is a good time for such a cold, astringent tonic.

The Journal Of A Disappointed Man was first published in March 1919, and on its last desperate page carried the italicised announcement that Barbellion, its remarkable author, had died on December 31, 1917— about two months after making the diary's last entry, which is the solitary word : 'Self-disgust.' Later it was found that this announcement was untrue, a curiously ill-advised piece of 'effectiveness' ; Barbellion was alive when his *Journal* appeared, and died on June 3rd, 1919. This was— from the detached point of view of readers of the *Journal*—a discouraging discovery, and could not but chill sympathy ; but the fact that he *did* live eighteen months longer than he, we must suppose, expected to—in pain, weakness and discomfort which it is torture to read about—was of ultimate great value, to him and to us ; for it gave him time to write *A Last Diary*, which is not nearly so well-known as the *Journal*, but which supplements and supports it—explaining, resolving much of the confused, knotted misery of the first book, and showing the disastrously unlucky man with his burden of wasted gifts and passionate regrets outgrowing, much more than the uneven courage of the *Journal* had shown him to, his terrible personal misery—and growing sweeter, lighter, truer and wittier in observation, gentler and more calm in habit of thought, as his body pressed home its violent defeat of him, and the real hour of his departure from it came in sight.

The two journals, read together, make a fine record—for they assemble *all* the essential truth about a personal tragedy which can be described as total. They take the unusually bright schoolboy—whose real name, by the way, was not Wilhelm Nero Pilate Barbellion but Bruce Frederick Cummings—with his spontaneous passion and genius for natural history from his poor and often happy days at home to the first chances, the successful examination, the post in the Natural History Museum, the stirrings of ambition, and then of love—to the premonitory encroachments of ill-health, and the beginning of a tragic, useless struggle. They give us truth about a love and a marriage, and show the goodness and necessity of that love as well as the doubts and second thoughts, not merely from the point of view of the diarist but, very justly and penetratingly, from the probable point of view of the girl who became his wife and bore him a child. They show all the theatre, all the self-pity, disgust and bewildered loneliness of a young, egoistical and brilliant man caught in a terrible trap ; but also they give flashes and passages of peace, that increase and grow truer as sorrow deepens, spreading at last to an almost constant witty sweetness, a near-gaiety, in *A Last Diary*. And because of this completion, because of the clear thinking, the control, the loving-kindness and the *fun* of the end, which justify and greatly ennoble him, we can surely rejoice a little in the hard extension by eighteen months of a life which—since by endowment he could have made it so fine—Barbellion had so often and so bitterly desired at an end.

He was very intelligent, in many directions. So his diaries, which exist to explain his personality and his fate to the world, as he intended them to, are not solely about himself, in the direct sense. They contain a great deal of objective observation of things and people, lively snatches of conversation, quick character-sketches and vigorous comment on books. And some of the best of these are in *A Last Diary*. His disrespectful admiration of Emily Brontë is amusingly expressed, for instance. 'One might almost write her down as Mrs Nietsche . . . no fit companion for the young ladies of a seminary. . . "No coward soul is mine" she tells us, with her fist held to our wincing nose.' In December 1918 he was writing : 'James Joyce is my man. Here is a writer who tells the truth about himself. It is almost impossible to tell the truth.' 'What I have always feared is coming to pass,' he says, with death well in sight, 'love for my little daughter. Only another communicating string with life to be cut.' 'I take my life in homeopathic doses now,' he says gently. Somewhere he says : 'Sir Thomas Browne was my father and Marie Bashkirtseff my mother.' It is an amusingly good shot. 'I am the scientific investigator of myself,' he says. He was greatly gifted ; and reading some of his character-impressions, and especially his conversations with his nurse towards the end, one feels that among the many things he might have done excellently the writing of novels was one.

It is curious that the last two diaries we shall speak of here, Barbellion's and Katherine Mansfield's, should be those of sick people, people doomed to die young and frustrated, and that, with Captain Scott's, their personal notes should stand for our century so far. But I cannot help the too-obvious symbolism ; it has worked out that way—and need not be taken too pessimistically. For all three were brave, exceptionally brave, and all were ultimate masters of their own tragedies, though we may proportion those tragedies as we choose in relation to universal things. Katherine

KATHERINE MANSFIELD, 1888-1923
Detail from an oil painting by Anne Estelle Rice

Mansfield's story needs no re-telling. She has left it to us in her work, in her letters, and in what she left undestroyed of her 'huge, complaining diaries.' That residue, published under the title of *Journal*, covers her life from 1914 to her death at Fontainebleau in October 1923. It is very personal, moody, self-pitying and brave. It contains notes for work, much discussion of work, sudden memories of childhood, outbursts of love, of gaiety and of desolation, and amusing, bitter, accomplished sketches of people encountered—and as it advances towards the darkness courage and ambitious desires rise up in greater waves, harder to meet, but which are met in fact by wisdom which has enlarged itself too, imperceptibly purified by detachment and humour—and by gentleness. The last pages of the *Journal* are clean of the occasional whimsicalities and false ironies that disfigure the earlier part; and there is a workmanlike, non-invalidish quality in the passages of rough notes, mere reminders for the professional —like the colour notes a painter makes. There is courage and goodness in this hard passion for work, and in the sick woman's lonely debates on the personal question of her illness and her love. And at the end she writes, thinking of another and of how to help him : 'And when I say "I fear" don't let it disturb you, dearest heart. We all fear when we are in waiting rooms. Yet we must pass beyond them, and if the other can keep calm, it is all the help we can give each other.'

Recollecting that I began this book by saying that the best English diaries have been written by bores, I can now only hope ruefully that I have not too much justified that sweeping statement. Yet I adhere to it—as I meant it ; *i.e.*, that the best and most typical English diarists would probably have been bores if they had not kept diaries—for they possessed that first attribute of the bore, the need to mention everything. And now, after much reading of diaries, and while allowing for all kinds of exceptions, the feeling I am left with is that the traditional, the generic English diary, from Pepys and Evelyn through the parsons and the political gossips to Crabb Robinson and Queen Victoria, is the escape, the safety-valve of the otherwise bore, the bright reverse of natural dullness.   Facts, actions, lists of things and people, details of movement, exact inform-ation, plain observation—all valuable and some enchanting, as it happens, after fifty or a hundred years—but *accidentally* so ; not designed expression, not making the exciting claims of works of art, but set down in routine, because of somebody's neat habit.   Lucky for us.   How much luckier we are, after all, to know Crabb Robinson in his diaries, as a whole, with all his illustrious friends massed about him on parade, than to have been mere acquaintances in his time of the busy, ubiquitous, unremarkable man with the absurdedly crowded engagement-book !

The women diarists are in a special case however. They are not as a genus bores *manquées*, because they very likely would not have been diarists if they could have been something more directly self-expressive. They are diarists *faute de mieux*, whether they knew it or not.   Dorothy Wordsworth kept journals and did no more creative writing only because, consciously or unconsciously, she had decided that devotion to William was her clearest and most necessary duty ; Fanny Burney wrote diaries because she should have been training herself to be a great novelist and had not enough decisiveness for that, so escaped, with ease and brilliance ; Miss Weeton wrote them because she was obscure and lost, half-mad with a sense of frustration, and the need to say something, somehow ; Caroline Fox was a natural intellectual who played second fiddle modestly to all her brilliant male friends.   And the Queen ? The Queen is above common rules, and in any case Victoria sweeps them away, as she should, by being perhaps at once a diarist *and* a bore.